Contents

Keymap

SCALE 1:312 500 or 1 INCH to 5 MILES *1CM to 3.1 KM*

0 2 4 6 8 10 KILOMETRES 15

0 2 4 6 MILES 8 10

KEYMAP HEIGHTS SHOWN IN FEET

Introduction

This is a walking book designed specifically for non-walkers; if that isn't a contradiction in terms. The 20 easy-to-follow routes have been carefully chosen to encourage inexperienced walkers to pull on a pair of boots and take their first few bold steps out into the joys and wonders of the great outdoors. To start with, on short and gentle strolls that the whole family will manage with ease and then, as the book progresses, on slightly more demanding jaunts that get deep into the heart of the wonderful Brecon Beacons' countryside but still won't take you more than half a day to complete.

Each outing has been selected for a specific reason; either because it visits a site of interest, or because it offers opportunities to see fascinating flora or fauna that otherwise wouldn't be seen, or, more often than not, just because it opens up some of the finest landscapes in the National Park and provides the walker with the kind of views that couldn't possibly be enjoyed from any car park or picnic site.

It's a book written with families in mind; each walk containing useful and interesting information about the area that it explores as well as including a specific question that will hopefully encourage the youngsters to play an active and inquisitive role in the day's proceedings.

The walks are graded by length and difficulty to allow the reader to choose the right one for the day and for the age and fitness level of the party that they are walking with. The easiest ones cross reasonably level ground on clear and easy-to-follow paths but this is very mountainous countryside and walks of this grade are hard to come by. Therefore most of the outings involve at least some uphill walking; the tougher ones, nearer the end of the book, a fair bit. Walk 20 is an ascent of the highest mountain in the National Park; a demanding ramble, yes, but also a worthwhile objective to work towards. Build up your fitness levels and experience gradually and never be afraid to back off a walk if anybody in the party is struggling or, as so often happens in these parts, the weather starts to deteriorate.

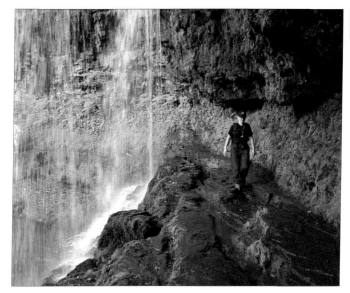

Sgwd yr Eira, Ystradfellte

Whilst specialist equipment isn't really necessary for any of these walks, a lot of them cross some very rough ground, as is often the way in mountainous terrain, so a pair of walking boots and some thick socks will certainly make things a lot more comfortable. On all but the shortest routes it's worth carrying a bottle of water and a few snacks. More than anything, these will offer comfort and encouragement to anybody who gets tired or cold.

The Brecon Beacons National Park

Covering an area of over 500 square miles, the Brecon Beacons National Park is actually made up of four distinct separate mountain ranges as well as some easier ground to the south and three isolated peaks that surround the small town of Abergavenny.

In the east, the Black Mountains comprise of five distinct broad ridges, linked at their northern end by some peaty moorland and an impressive north-facing escarpment that casts a lengthy shadow over the wide expanse of the Wye Valley. Walk 13, a straightforward sortie around the head of the Grwyne Fawr Valley, penetrates deep into the heart of this range, whilst Walk 18 traces the Cat's Back along its easternmost reaches. Walks 10, 11 and 18 all offer fantastic views of the range.

South of these hills are the three Abergavenny peaks. The highest, the Sugar Loaf, is one of the most distinctive mountains in the area and is explored in Walk 17, whilst across the Usk Valley stands the imposing bulk of the mighty Blorenge, a lofty peak that's easily scaled by Walk 11. The third, Ysgyryd Fawr isn't covered in the book but is well worth a visit.

The skyline in the centre of the National Park is dominated by the Brecon Beacons themselves, whose dramatic profiles are at their most impressive when viewed from the north on Walk 7; an easy stroll across Mynydd Illtud Common. Their southern slopes present a friendlier face to walkers who follow Walk 4 and Walk 15, and their summits are crested by the toughest route in the book on Walk 20.

The Cat's Back, Olchon Valley, Black Mountains

West of the true Beacons is Fforest Fawr, once the hunting ground of kings, now a windswept cluster of grassy topped peaks that don't lend themselves to easy family walking. An exception is Craig Cerrig-gleisiad – a National Nature Reserve. Its deep hollows and craggy tops are examined close-up on Walk 12. South of these mountains, the rivers have carved deep gorges for themselves and it's here that the most impressive waterfalls in the National Park are found. Walk 16 takes a ramble around these.

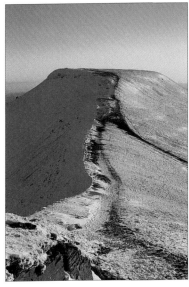

Pen y Fan in winter

The far west is known as the Mynydd Du or Black Mountain (singular) and this is probably the most remote part of the National Park, comprising of mile after mile of austere moorland that sees far fewer visitors than the other areas. Even this forbidding landscape has its weaknesses though, and Walk 9 gets deep into its bosom with minimum effort, as it climbs to the scenic and now legendary Llyn y Fan Fach, a beautiful mountain tarn nestled beneath towering cliffs. Walk 6 skirts around the edge of the wilderness – starting at the lovely Craig-y-nos Country Park – and Walk 19 allows some clear views of its magnificent skyline from the wooded shores of this area's largest stretch of water.

From gurgling brook to turbulent river, from sheltered glade to windswept summit and from rolling meadow to sprawling forest, there really is something here for everybody. History abounds, wildlife ekes a living out of every nook and cranny and even the scars of the industrial revolution have left a unique yet attractive mark on this very special corner of Wales. The aim of this book is to help you to enjoy it.

1 Blaen-y-glyn

START Pont Blaen-y-glyn
(grid ref: SO 062170)
DISTANCE 1½ miles
(2.4km)
TIME 1 hour
PARKING Car park next to
the bridge
ROUTE FEATURES
Woodland; tree roots;
muddy paths; slippery
rocks

This is a lovely and straightforward walk through pretty woodland and along the banks of a wonderful mountain stream, peppered with spectacular cascades and waterfalls. The going does get quite rough in some places and a few sections of the path can be quite muddy. Boots are definitely recommended for keeping feet dry.

Walk up through the car park, away from the road, on a good firm track that leads into the woods. Continue easily upwards past some wonderful moss-covered tumbledown walls and across a few small streams.

Keep heading in the same direction until you cross a small bridge that spans a turbulent stream, with some small cascades above and below you **Ⓐ**. Turn left after the bridge and start heading upstream with the stream on your left. As the path bends to the right and starts to

climb very steeply, you can keep ahead to follow the stream into an almost magical grotto with a wonderful waterfall directly ahead. *The path is usually muddy here and the rocks are very slippery.*

Return to the woodland path, where if you wish, you can turn left to continue steeply uphill to view further waterfalls. If you don't fancy the steep climb, turn right to retrace your steps back to the main path, where you need to turn left for a few paces to a fork, with some ruined buildings to your left.

PUBLIC TRANSPORT Summer bus service from Brecon and Talybont on Usk
REFRESHMENTS None
PUBLIC TOILETS None
ORDNANCE SURVEY MAPS Explorer OL12 (Brecon Beacons Western & Central areas), Landranger 160 (Brecon Beacons)

Turn right at the fork and drop down to a stile that leads to a bridge over the Caerfanell River **B**. Here you'll get your first sighting of the spectacular Caerfanell Falls.

The walk continues over the bridge but before crossing, it is possible to make your way up the rocky bank towards the falls to get a better view. *Care is needed; the rock is usually quite slippery.* Now cross the bridge and turn left to follow a

Backlit leaves and rocks, Blaen-y-glyn

Fast flowing rivers and streams like the Caerfanell are great places to spot wildlife. There are many different species of birds and mammals making the banks and surrounding woodland their home. These include **otters**, which are very secretive and seldom seen, and **mink**, which are not indigenous but have spread across most of the UK.

narrow and often muddy path upstream a few metres to look at the top of the falls. Return to the bridge and keep straight ahead,

? *Pont is the Welsh word for bridge. How many bridges do you cross on the walk?*

now with the stream to your right. Navigation is easy from here as all you need to do is follow the river-bank down, enjoying the many rapids and cascades as you go.

There's plenty to look out for.

Dippers are frequently seen dashing from rock to rock in the stream and you may also spot grey wagtails or even the odd heron. *The path is tricky in places, with a few steep and slippery sections that need to be treated with care.* Eventually the going eases and you're left with an easy short stroll to the bridge. Go through the kissing-gate and turn right to cross the river and return to the car park.

Caerfanell waterfall

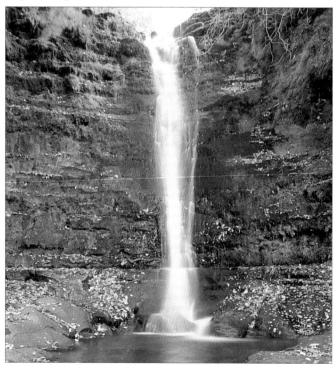

Castle Meadows

2

START Abergavenny bus station
 (grid ref: SO 300140)
DISTANCE 1½ miles (2.4km)
TIME 1 hour
PARKING Pay and Display at the start
ROUTE FEATURES Clear paths; grassy meadows; riverside path; castle ruins; museum

An easy and enjoyable stroll; suitable for the whole family and easily accessible by public transport. Abergavenny makes a great base for exploration; particularly of the Black Mountains area. This walk traces the banks of the mighty River Usk as it brushes up against the bustling little market town. As well as providing a good chance to spot wildlife, it also offers great views of the surrounding mountains. Leave plenty of time to explore the castle and museum too.

Walk past the information centre and out of the car park onto the road. Turn right and then cross the road immediately to turn left, up Mill Street, with the Shahi Indian restaurant on your right. As the road veers left, keep ahead until the road ends and a path leads you down to Castle Meadows. The castle walls can be seen on top of the large hillock on the right.

Turn left at a fancy waymark post **A** and walk down to the gate that leads out onto the meadows. Go

through this and bear right to follow a muddy path towards a

Little more than a tumbledown ruin in a prominent position overlooking the River Usk, **Abergavenny Castle** was originally founded in the 11th century. The stone construction that we see now was started in the later 1100s by the Normans and added to until it reached its most impressive condition during the 13th and 14th century. It was visited by King John in 1215. Charles I ordered its demolition in 1645 when it became a good source for local building stone.

PUBLIC TRANSPORT Buses and trains to Abergavenny
REFRESHMENTS The walk can be broken up by visiting the Bridge End Inn, Llanfoist, which is a few minutes from **B**. Abergavenny has plenty of cafés
PUBLIC TOILETS At the start
ORDNANCE SURVEY MAPS Explorer OL13 (Brecon Beacons Eastern area), Landranger 161 (The Black Mountains)

Abergavenny Castle

wooden bridge, keeping a boggy dyke to your right. Cross the bridge and keep heading in the same direction to cross the meadows until you reach a well-surfaced track that crosses your path. Keep ahead here, still on the muddy path, and continue until you reach the far side of the meadows, where you'll clearly see the road ahead **B**.

Turn left to keep the wall to your right and walk down to join a well-surfaced trail at an elaborate kissing-gate. Turn left onto this trail and

? *What is the name for Abergavenny in Welsh?*

follow it along the banks of the river with fine views over the water to the steep slopes of the Blorenge mountain. After a few minutes, you'll notice some sandy cliffs on the opposite bank. In summer, this makes a great nesting area for sand martins, which burrow into the bank and can be seen catching flies above the river.

Waymark near Abergavenny Castle

Continue until the main path veers to the left **C** but keep straight ahead, again on a muddy path, to follow the riverbank a little farther. Soon you'll cross a wooden footbridge over a small tributary stream and then, just a few paces farther on, you'll be forced to keep left to follow another stream up towards another footbridge **D**. This stream is actually the Gavenny River, from which the town takes its name.

Don't cross this bridge, which is now on your right. Instead, bear left to join a good path and follow this back to another bridge, where you bear right, through a gate. Follow the grassy track up to the elaborate waymark that you passed earlier at **A**. To return to the car park, turn right to retrace your steps. *To visit the castle and museum, keep ahead now, with the castle walls above you to your right, and continue up to the gates on the right. When you've finished, retrace your steps back down to the waymark to return to the car park.* ●

3 St Mary's Vale

START Head of narrow lane near Abergavenny (grid ref: SO 283161)

DISTANCE 1¾ miles (2.8km)

TIME 1 hour

PARKING At the start

ROUTE FEATURES Woodland; tree roots; stream crossings; slippery rocks; steep climb; open hillsides

One of the prettiest wooded valleys in the area, St Mary's Vale provides enjoyable and energetic walking on the outskirts of Abergavenny. In spring, the sound of birdsong fills the air and in autumn the colours are truly wonderful. Some of the paths can be difficult to follow in late summer when the bracken is high.

Walk out of the car park and turn left for a few paces to a fork. Keep left to walk along a gravel drive that runs beneath a house to a gate. Go through the gate and drop down a clear track to the stream at the bottom of the valley. Cross the flagstone bridge **A** but don't be tempted over the stile on the left, instead, keep the stream to your left and walk up into the woods.

Cross a narrow channel so that you are walking with the stream on both sides and then cross it again so that the stream is now on your right. You are on a clear jeep track that continues up into woods. Stay with this until it makes a sharp left hairpin turn by a broader pool in the stream **B**. Cross the stream here and you will see two paths forking up the hillside. Take the left-hand one, and climb steeply, on a clear but narrow path away from the stream. Eventually the path levels at an open glade, just short of some open hillside, with a fence corner to the right and a huge oak tree marking a junction of tracks **C**.

Bear left, around the oak tree, and walk beneath a fallen branch on a

PUBLIC TRANSPORT None

REFRESHMENTS None

PUBLIC TOILETS None

ORDNANCE SURVEY MAPS Explorer OL13 (Brecon Beacons Eastern area), Landranger 161 (The Black Mountains)

narrow path that soon meets a brook. Keep the brook to your left and continue for a few paces to an obvious crossing point on the edge of open ground. There's a small sign pointing right but you need to keep straight ahead on a clear track that swings slightly right and continues up through the heather and bilberry. You'll soon come to a three-way fork, with an animal drinking trough to your left and a

path that leads to a stile to your right. Ignore these and keep straight ahead to merge with a clearer track that comes in from your left.

Shortly after this, the track levels again and you'll see a fence to your

Much of the land on this walk belongs to the **National Trust**, an independent charity that owns nearly 250,000 hectares of land in Wales, England and Northern Ireland. Founded over a century ago by three philanthropists – Miss Octavia Hill, Sir Robert Hunter and Canon Hardwicke Rawnsley, its role is to acquire and protect coastline, countryside and buildings for the nation to enjoy. It actually owns over 3500 ha (9000 acres) of the land in the National Park.

right . Now follow the path downhill, keeping the fence to your right and the open hillside to your left all the time. You'll soon enter the wood again where the path widens into a broad terraced track that passes a bench on the left. Continue easily down to a gate and keep straight ahead to drop back to the car park.

Autumn birch trees

Coed Taf Fawr

4

START Garwnant Forest Park (grid ref: SO 002131)
DISTANCE 2 miles (3.2km)
TIME 1 hour
PARKING Pay and Display at the start
ROUTE FEATURES Forest trails; muddy paths; tree roots; stream crossing; waterfalls

Garwnant Forest Park is one of the real highlights of the area, especially for families, and this walk, an easy waymarked stroll from the superbly equipped visitor centre, is a great introduction. Known as the Wern Walk, it follows the long distance Taff Trail past the derelict buildings of Wern Farm before climbing up onto a broad forest track for an easy return leg.

Make your way over towards the rope course and then, facing it, with the visitor centre down to your right, bear left, to follow a Taff Trail waymark away from the car park and onto a broad forest track. Look for waymark posts with green arrows, which will guide you all the way round. Now

Witches' butter on a dead tree

follow this trail easily along, through a variety of different woodland, until you reach the derelict buildings of Wern Farm **Ⓐ**.

> **?** *What is special about coniferous trees?*

PUBLIC TRANSPORT Bus service from Brecon and Merthyr Tydfil
REFRESHMENTS Café at the visitor centre
PUBLIC TOILETS At the start
PICNIC/PLAY AREA Elaborate play area at the start
ORDNANCE SURVEY MAPS Explorer OL12 (Brecon Beacons Western & Central areas), Landranger 160 (Brecon Beacons)

Forest track and trees

Keep these to your left and continue, now on a narrow and sometimes muddy track. A few more minutes of easy walking will see you arrive at a small brook crossing and then, shortly after that, you'll come to a crossroads of tracks **B**, where you need to keep straight ahead although the Taff Trail now drops down to the right to carry on up the Taf Fawr Valley towards Brecon.

Keep heading in the same direction and you'll soon come to some tumbledown buildings, where the trail turns sharp left to go uphill. Follow the trail up, with a tumbling brook down to your right, and beyond that, a recently harvested section of woodland stretching away towards Nant-ddu. At the top of this section, you'll meet a broad well-

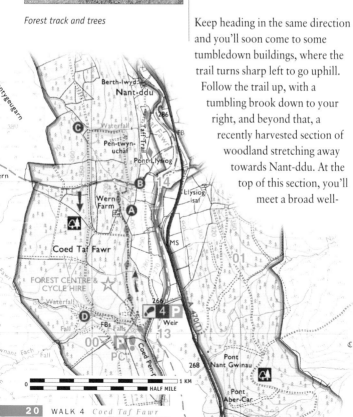

surfaced forest road **C**, and another waymarker post with a green arrow.

Turn left onto this and follow it easily along, with good views in all directions. You'll soon cross the bridleway track that you crossed on the way out and then, shortly after that, you'll pass another forest track that dips off to the left. Continue to a junction **D**, where you start to drop into a valley, and bear left here, to start heading downhill with the powerful Garwnant River down to your right. There are some spectacular falls all the way down the river, which soon finishes its journey as it

Garwnant Forest Park is a wonderful facility for all the family with waymarked forest walks, family cycle trails and even an adventure playground, which includes a rope course and a toddlers' play area. The visitor centre features interesting displays and has a gift shop, a café that serves great food made from local produce, and a cosy log fire. Cycle hire is also available if you'd rather ride than walk.

flows into the Afon Taf Fawr, near the Llwyn-on Reservoir.

Continue on down until you see a good path on your left that leads you back up to the car park and visitor centre.

Derelict building, Coed Taf Fawr

5 *Tor y Foel*

START Small parking area above Talybont-on-Usk (grid ref: SO 109187)
DISTANCE 2¼ miles (3.6km)
TIME 1½ hours
PARKING At the start
ROUTE FEATURES Grassy tracks; muddy paths; views; steep descent

A short but wonderfully rewarding walk that crosses some remote moorland before climbing steeply up onto one of the best viewpoints in the National Park. Save this one for a good day as navigation would be awkward in poor visibility and you'd also miss out on the fabulous views across the surrounding countryside.

There's room for a few cars by the gate at the top of the farm drive. From here, walk left, for a few yards, to the corner of the wall and start up the obvious path that climbs the steep grassy slopes of the mountain. After just a few paces, turn right to join a faint path that traverses around the hillside, with the wall down to your right.

? *You can see the Talybont Reservoir from the walk; what's the difference between a reservoir and a lake?*

Continue around, rising up slightly to pass the corner of a wood **Ⓐ**. Keep heading in the same direction and shortly the heather and bilberry gives way to a fairly thick carpet of bracken, which makes the path difficult to see in mid to late summer. Continue on the same line, with the steep slope to your left and the wall down to your right, and the way ahead should become clear. This is a good place to see mountain birds like the skylark and meadow pipit, which both enjoy this kind of open hillside. In autumn and winter, the

PUBLIC TRANSPORT None
REFRESHMENTS None
PUBLIC TOILETS None
ORDNANCE SURVEY MAPS Explorer OL13 (Brecon Beacons Eastern area), Landranger 161 (The Black Mountains)

area is regularly visited by huge flocks of redwings and fieldfares, which feed off the berries on the

Looking over Bwlch-y-waun from Tor y Foel

numerous small trees that cover the slopes.

Eventually you'll reach flatter ground and the bracken thins out slightly, revealing some peculiar bumpy ground. Bear left here and climb easily up onto the crest of the hill, where you'll meet the obvious main track that runs up the eastern ridge of the mountain **B**.

Turn left onto this and take your time as you pull steeply up towards the top. The views are magnificent, with the Usk Valley down to your right; the mighty river snaking along its floor, and beyond this, the Black Mountains rise up in all their splendour. Southwards you look

Tor y Foel from Allt Lwyd

over the deeply cloven valley of the Dyffryn Crawnon to the austere slopes of Mynydd Llangynidr.

From the top **C**, you'll see right across the Caerfanell Valley to the moorland plateau of Waun Rhydd, towering above the glistening waters of the Talybont Reservoir. There's scant shelter at the summit so unless it's a particularly good day, you'll probably want to get moving straight away. Drop down the obvious path, and continue steeply down with great views now over the head of Caerfanell Valley to the outlying peak of Allt Lwyd. Continue all the way back down to the road, where you left the car.

> The **Talybont Reservoir** was originally constructed in the 1930s. It took a considerable work force to build the impressive dam and over 200 people were forced to move home as the valley was flooded. It is now a **Site of Specific Interest (SSI)** and an important habitat for wildfowl. The dam can be crossed on foot or bicycle.

Craig-y-nos and the Tawe Valley

6

START Craig-y-nos Country Park (grid ref: SN 839155)
DISTANCE 2½ miles (4km)
TIME 1½ hours
PARKING Pay and Display at the start
ROUTE FEATURES Muddy paths; riverside; stepping stones; field paths; road crossings

This is a gem of a walk that follows the mighty Tawe River from Craig-y-nos Country Park to its confluence with the equally impressive Afon Haffes, which drains from the dramatic heights of the Black Mountain. The going is easy the whole way round, although some athleticism might be needed to cross the stepping stones over the Afon Haffes.

Walk down the path that leads from the car park and go through the gap in the wall to the shores of the pool. Turn right here and follow the gravel track down and around to a wooden bridge that crosses the Afon Tawe. Cross the bridge and bear left to follow a lovely path upstream with a clearing on your right. Continue into a stand of large pine trees and keep ahead until you meet a wooden fence where the path leaves the country park and joins a bridleway on the banks of the river

Mute swan and Craig-y-nos Country Park

PUBLIC TRANSPORT Regular bus service between Brecon and Swansea
REFRESHMENTS The walk passes the Gwyn Arms. Vending machine at the visitor centre
PUBLIC TOILETS At the start
PICNIC/PLAY AREA Near the start, where there's also a duck pond. Dan-yr-ogof Showcaves on the walk
ORDNANCE SURVEY MAPS Explorer OL12 (Brecon Beacons Western & Central areas), Landranger 160 (Brecon Beacons)

A . Keep ahead to cross a bridge and then continue along the path, going through a gate and between trees to another gate. Continue to the main road **B** .

Cross the road and hop over the stile opposite to walk up the edge of the field with the fence to your right. Go over another stile at the top and then another, that leads onto the drive of Dan-yr-ogof Showcaves. Turn right and follow the metalled drive down to a junction, where you keep straight ahead, over a stile, to continue on a good track. Look for a waymark that directs you leftwards, uphill on a rough track. Follow this to a gate and keep ahead to join another track after a few paces. Turn right here and drop down to the Afon Haffes **C** .

The riverbanks are a jumble of stones and boulders so do your best to cross the river using these and then keep ahead to a gate and stile that lead into a copse of hazel and birch. Follow the track easily along, with open mountainside to your left and the copse to your right. Bear around to the right, to cross a number of stiles and pass a house, which you keep to your left. Continue to the road **D** .

Turn left to walk along the broad verge and then, cross to continue in the same

The Victorian **Craig-y-nos Estate** was **originally built in 1840**. In 1878, Adelina Patti, a top opera singer bought the estate and extended both the house and gardens to create a wonderful retreat. After her death in 1919, the house became a hospital. The beautiful grounds are now managed by the Brecon Beacons National Park as a country park with a small but informative visitor centre.

direction on the pavement. Turn right, through a kissing-gate, into the churchyard and then follow the path around the back of the church to another kissing-gate. Keep ahead to cross a lane and go through another kissing-gate to walk up a field with an old wall to your right. At the top of this field, bear diagonally right to cross the next to a gate by the houses **E**. Turn left onto the road and drop to

cross a bridge before climbing for a few more paces to a kissing-gate on your right.

Go through this and follow the wall along to a gate. Open this and keep the wall to your left now to pass a huge crater to another gate. Head diagonally upwards to a gate at the top, where you join a sunken bridleway track **F**. Turn right onto this and follow it easily for ½ mile (800m) to a gate. Go through this and drop to a small gate on your right, open it and you'll be back on the banks of the Afon Tawe. Turn left to retrace your steps back to the start.

What kind of horses are kept in the centre that you walk past?

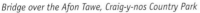
Bridge over the Afon Tawe, Craig-y-nos Country Park

7 *Mynydd Illtud*

START Mountain centre, Libanus
(grid ref: SN 978262)
DISTANCE 2¾ miles (4.4km)
TIME 1½ hours
PARKING Pay and Display at the start
ROUTE FEATURES Grassy tracks; views; ponds; Iron Age fort

Although very easy, this is one of the most rewarding walks in the whole book. It follows gently undulating grassy tracks across the common land of Mynydd Illtud and terminates on the ramparts of an Iron Age fort that offers breathtaking views across the highest mountains in the National Park. Allow time to investigate the displays in the mountain centre and to enjoy lunch in the excellent restaurant.

Walk up through the car park, away from the buildings, to a stile that leads out onto the common. There are a few tracks and paths radiating out from here but you need to take the main one, that goes straight ahead, climbing ever so slightly and running parallel with the fence, which is 50 yds (46m) below you to your right. This track does get closer to the fence after a few minutes but it then climbs away from it again before a major junction **Ⓐ**, where you should be able to see a pond ahead and to your right. Keep straight ahead here, keeping to the main path rather than dropping to the pond, and continue past the pond, to another junction, just a few metres short of the narrow road.

Bear diagonally right here to drop to the road by a white post that marks a pipeline. Cross the road and continue in the same direction, following a good path that runs along the edge of the common,

PUBLIC TRANSPORT Beacon Buses summer service from Brecon. Year round buses stop at the bottom of the lane in Libanus, 2km from the start
REFRESHMENTS Excellent restaurant at the mountain centre
PUBLIC TOILETS At the start
PICNIC/PLAY AREA At the start
ORDNANCE SURVEY MAPS Explorer OL12 (Brecon Beacons Western & Central areas), Landranger 160 (Brecon Beacons)

with a wall to your right. Stay with this and drop to another narrow lane **B**. You can now see Twyn y Gaer, the hill you are going to climb, directly ahead. Cross the road and keep straight ahead to continue along the edge of the common. Shortly, you'll pass a small pond on your right and then, a few paces after this, you'll see a clear track leading uphill towards the summit of the hill. Follow this up to the trig point **C**. This is a wonderful viewpoint with Pen y Fan and Corn Du, the highest mountains in the whole of southern Britain, clearly visible. In the distance, you'll make out the

Pen y Fan and Corn Du from Mynydd Illtud

> **?** *Why did the Iron Age people build their settlements on the tops of hills?*

dark shapes of the northern slopes of the Black Mountains and due north; you'll see the River Usk snaking along the valley floor beneath your feet.

To return, bear left at the trig point, to drop down the centre of the ridge on a good clear grassy path that leads back to the road. Cross this and follow the waymark that directs you up and over the next hill. Continue to the road and keep straight ahead again, to follow the main track for approximately 100 yds (92m) to the junction where you turned right earlier. Bear diagonally right here, onto a clear and dead straight track that climbs slightly. Follow

Mynydd Illtud Common is now a nature reserve, but this area was once common land, as designated by the manorial system introduced by the Normans. This system gave common people certain rights including grazing, fishing, peat digging and removal of stone, mineral and soil. The lord of the manor retained the hunting and shooting rights. Today, common land is mainly used for grazing and recreation, and this is protected by law. Mynydd Illtud is actually owned by the National Park Authority.

this until the track meets the road, by a large pond. Now bear left, towards some uneven ground on the other side of the pond, and follow the track easily downhill, back to the mountain centre. ●

Mynydd Illtud and the mountains of Fforest Fawr

Gilwern Wharf and the Clydach Gorge

START Gilwern Wharf
(grid ref: SO 242147)
DISTANCE 2¼ miles
(3.6km)
TIME 1½ hours
PARKING Gilwern Wharf
ROUTE FEATURES Canal
towpath; steep muddy
track; quiet lanes; grassy
footpaths; woodland path

Often overlooked by visitors to the National Park, the area around Gilwern and the Clydach Gorge boasts a fascinating past, evidence of which can still be found amongst some quite magnificent scenery. This lovely and straightforward walk links the serenity of the Brecon and Monmouthshire Canal with the beautiful wooded valley of the Clydach Gorge, visiting a wonderfully situated church along the way. Although most of the walk is on good paths, the steep climb away from the canal can get muddy at times.

From the car park, continue along the canal side, shortly passing a bridge with a seat above it that offers great views over the Black Mountains. Continue to the next bridge, number 106, **A** and walk beneath this before crossing the stone stile on your right. Turn right to double back on yourself and cross the bridge – note the old

sign – and then follow the track up through trees where it becomes a sunken green lane. Continue up the steep hill until it finally levels and spills onto the road near Llanelly church **B**.

Originally built in the early 13th-century, the church, which occupies a marvellous position with wonderful views, was added

PUBLIC TRANSPORT Buses from Abergavenny
REFRESHMENTS The Corn Exchange at Gilwern is close to the start. The Bridge Inn is also a few minutes from the route at the end. There's also a tearoom in the antique shop in Gilwern
PUBLIC TOILETS None
PICNIC/PLAY AREA Picnic area at the start
ORDNANCE SURVEY MAPS Explorer OL13 (Brecon Beacons Eastern area), Landranger 161 (The Black Mountains)

hedgerow on your right as you follow the field edge down to a stile. Cross this and turn right onto a broad farm track, which you follow to a narrow lane. Turn left and drop down to a crossroads ⒞ where you need to keep straight ahead and walk steeply downhill.

Follow the road down past Clydach House and around to the

Cascades in the Clydach Gorge

to in 1626, possibly funded by the new found local wealth, courtesy of the Clydach Iron Works.

Turn left and walk down the road for a few paces to a stile on the right. Cross this and walk through the middle of the field to another stile, marked 'footpath' and cross this to continue in the same direction. The next stile leads into the corner of a field, where you should keep straight ahead, with the fence to your left, on a slightly raised walkway. Bear right upon reaching the far corner of the field and then cross a stile on the left. Now bear right to keep the

Brecon and Monmouthshire Canal, Gilwern

left. At the bottom of the hill, turn left onto a narrow lane that was once the Llam March tram road. Follow this past a row of cottages, once forge workers' dwellings, to the gate to Forge House **D**. Go through the gate and keep straight ahead, with the house to your right. Beyond this, you'll see a narrow path leading away between

> **?** *What do you call a bridge that carries water? (Look at the cottage close to this bridge.)*

hedges. Follow this down into woodland and continue along the banks of the Clydach River, still on the line of the old tram road, passing a bridge on the right. Keep straight ahead at the fork and continue until the narrow wooded track emerges onto a broader track. Turn right and walk downhill, beneath the aquaduct that carries the canal, and then climb the steps on the other side.

At the top, turn right onto the canal and follow the towpath back under a bridge to the wharf. ●

> The **Llam March tram road** was **built in 1809** to link the Clydach Ironworks with the Brecon and Monmouthshire Canal. As you approach the canal, you'll see the Clydach Railroad that runs above you to the left. This is now the road that leads up the gorge, through Maes-y-gwartha. The tram road joins the canal at the Clydach Basin, which is now a boatyard for a narrowboat company.

9 *Llyn y Fan Fach*

START Small car park west of Llanddeusant (grid ref: SN 798238)
DISTANCE 2½ miles (4km)
TIME 1½ hours
PARKING At the start, busy on good days, get there early
ROUTE FEATURES Rocky track; lakeside mountain views

The lofty escarpments of the Carmarthen Fan are generally out of bounds to the casual walker but there is one weakness in their defence; an old waterworks track that leads up to Llyn y Fan Fach; often referred to as the 'magic lake' and one of the most scenic spots in the west of the National Park.

From the car park, join the rocky track and turn right to walk over a bridge and around to the right. Navigation is easy from this point onwards so just stay on the track, with the tumbling Afon Sawdde to your right, and climb gradually upstream until you reach the fish farm at about half distance **Ⓐ**. The way ahead is blocked by a gate so bear left, through a gap in the wall, and then turn right to follow a narrow and rough path past the old filter beds, which are now used as a fish hatchery so you'll spot plenty of jumping fish.

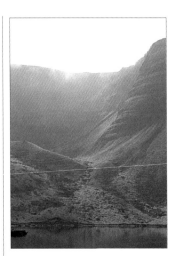

Bannau Sir Gaer

PUBLIC TRANSPORT None
REFRESHMENTS None
PUBLIC TOILETS None
ORDNANCE SURVEY MAPS Explorer OL12 (Brecon Beacons Western & Central areas), Landranger 160 (Brecon Beacons)

As well as occupying a stunning position beneath the broken brags of Bannau Sir Gaer, **Llyn y Fan Fach** is also **steeped in myths and legends**, the most famous concerning a magical 'Lady of the Lake'. Legend tells of a local shepherd boy named Rhiwallon who saw the beautiful lady rise from the still waters of the lake. He instantly fell in love with her and asked her to marry him, which she agreed to do so long as he never struck her with iron. They lived happily together. He tended his animals and she produced all kinds of magical healing potions from local herbs and flowers, a skill that she later passed on to their son. Sadly, he did eventually strike her with iron and, true to her word, she returned to the waters of the lake, taking their livestock with her and leaving Rhiwallon a broken man. The son went on to become the first of a line of healers now known as the **Physicians of Myddfai**.

Continue until the path drops down to join the main track again and follow this on upwards to a bridge that crosses the Afon Sawdde. Keep heading up, with the water now down to your left, and after another few minutes, you'll see a fork, with a grassy path leading off to the left. Take this and follow it around a steep bank to the grassy shores of the reservoir **B**. The steep cliffs ahead are known as the Carmarthen Fans, with the mountain directly above the lake known as Bannau Sir Gaer. Beyond this, and out of sight, the open moorland of the Black Mountain becomes increasingly wild and untrodden.

It's possible to walk most of the way around the lake and there are some great places to enjoy lunch surrounded by some of the finest mountain scenery in the whole of Wales. To return, locate the small hut, which is now an emergency shelter, and follow the track away from this. It goes around a sharp left-hand bend and then bears down to the right, where you'll see the fork that you took earlier. Now continue back down, retracing your steps past the fish farm and back down to the car park.

How many fish can you see jumping from the hatchery pools?

The Carmarthen Fan and Llyn y Fan Fach

The Llangattock Escarpment

A straightforward ramble that offers some fantastic views as well as an insight into the huge quarrying industry that once dominated the hillsides in this part of Wales. The craggy escarpments of Craig y Cilau are breathtakingly grand and the towering limestone cliffs are home to all kinds of wildlife.

START Car park on Llangattock Escarpment (grid ref: SO 208154)

DISTANCE 3¼ miles (5.2km)

TIME 2 hours

PARKING Car park at start

ROUTE FEATURES Grassy tracks; steep paths; spectacular cliff scenery; views; industrial history

10

Walk out of the car park and back down the access track to the road. Turn left and follow this along to some cottages on your left. Keep straight ahead as the road veers round to the right, and continue past the final cottage and out onto the open hillside on a broad grassy track that was once a tram road used for carrying limestone from the quarries above. Continue easily along until after a couple of grass-covered piles of spoil on the right, the track narrows considerably and you can see a built-up platform on your right **A**.

Turn right here and descend steeply to the corner of the wood below. Here you'll see the remains of an old wheelman's hut and also a park bench, that offers fine views over the Usk Valley. Turn left here onto a narrow but clear path that is often covered by bracken in the summer. Follow it uphill slightly at first and then contour around the hillside, with great views ahead to the imposing cliffs of Craig y Cilau. The path then drops to the banks of a small stream that emerges from a wall on the floor of the valley **B**.

PUBLIC TRANSPORT None
REFRESHMENTS None
PUBLIC TOILETS None
ORDNANCE SURVEY MAPS Explorer OL13 (Brecon Beacons Eastern area), Landranger 161 (The Black Mountains)

? **What's wrong with the name of the cottage near the start of the walk?**

Turn left and keep the wall to your right to walk along a rough path that climbs steadily upwards. Continue for nearly one mile (1.6km), passing the nature reserve boundary, and then, as you divert left, to pass the very obvious corner

Iron rafter, ruined quarry buildings, Llangattock

of a wall, keep your eyes open to your left for a faint narrow path that cuts back very sharply to start up the steep hillside **C**. There is actually a small marker post on the left but this is often covered by bracken.

The path is narrow and reasonably level to start with but it soon steepens and climbs stiffly to a grassy bank with a marker post on it. Keep ahead to continue upwards until you eventually reach a good level track. This is another of the old tram roads that was used to transport the limestone from the quarries. To your right, 300 yds (274m) farther on, is Ogof Agen Allwedd, the entrance to one of the longest cave systems in Britain. You turn left however, and follow the easy track eastwards past a sign for the nature reserve. Continue for

Crickhowell from the Llangattock Escarpment

100 yds (92m) beyond this and then fork right on to an obvious but narrow path that leads up onto a plateau dotted with small piles of spoil **D**.

Follow the narrow path as it undulates along with the cliffs uphill to your right. Keep right at any forks and eventually you'll find yourself on a clearer, broader track that heads leftwards around the huge banks of spoil at Chwar Pant-y-Rhiw. Continue until a good track joins from the right. This comes through the cutting between the banks and the quarry faces. Now, at the next fork, bear left, to follow a good firm track downwards to a junction of tracks **E**. A brief detour to the right will expose a lime kiln and tumbledown quarry building. Keep ahead, still on a good track and this will drop you back easily to the car park. ●

As well as boasting some of the best views in the whole National Park, the **Llangattock Escarpment** conceals some wonderful **industrial history**. The limestone escarpment was quarried from the early 19th-century, if not earlier, and the tracks that this walk follows were once all part of the sophisticated transport network used to get the quarried stone and lime down to the Brecon and Monmouthshire Canal, near Llangattock village. The building at the top of the steep path at **A** was once a wheelhouse and the steep path, an incline down which the stone was lowered. The flat, broad tram ways now make wonderful footpaths and the grass-covered spoil heaps only add to the overall atmosphere.

11 *The Blorenge*

START Carn-y-gorfydd
Roadside Rest
(grid ref: SO 270109)
DISTANCE 3½ miles
(5.6km)
TIME 2 hours
PARKING Car park at start
ROUTE FEATURES Grassy
tracks; muddy paths;
views; rocky summit;
quiet road section

The imposing bulk of the Blorenge towers above Abergavenny offering surprisingly easy walking as well as wonderful views across the small town to the sprawling massif of the Black Mountains. This walk uses broad, easy-to-follow tracks to explore the mountain's impressive north-facing escarpment and to cross its austere summit plateau. There are also some great places to have a picnic.

Leave the car park and follow the narrow lane downhill for 300 yds (274m) to a grassy track on the left, guarded by a green-painted barrier. Go around this and follow the track steeply uphill with the views over the Usk Valley opening up all the time as you go. Stay with it all the way to the top, passing some grassy banks created by quarrying spoil, until you reach a small brick hut **A** that marks the start of the path up towards the summit. For now though, continue around the escarpment edge, with the drop into the valley to your right. This offers some wonderful views across Abergavenny to the Sugar Loaf and also to the Black Mountains, farther west. Continue around the escarpment as far as you wish. The small rocky outcrops that crown the steep hillside provide plenty of shelter so the grassy terraces between make perfect, very scenic picnic spots.

This mountain is very popular with hang-gliders and paragliders, who make the most of the up-draughts to fly out above the Usk Valley.

PUBLIC TRANSPORT None
REFRESHMENTS None
PUBLIC TOILETS None
ORDNANCE SURVEY MAPS Explorer OL13 (Brecon Beacons Eastern area),
Landranger 161 (The Black Mountains)

gives you access to the true summit plateau **Ⓑ**. This was once the most southerly of Britain's managed grouse moors and you are still very likely to see or even hear red grouse as you walk along this section; listen out for their disgruntled calls that at times actually sound as if they are saying 'get back, get back!'

Continue along the main track to the rocky top; crowned with a whitewashed trig point. The

The Blorenge

When you've finished your exploration, return to the small brick hut, and turn right, to follow a vague track up the hill above it. Cross a short boggy patch and then climb a short steep stretch that

Britain won just one gold medal in the 1952 Olympic Games, held in Helsinki, and that was in the show jumping, where **Welshman Sir Harry Llewellyn** rode a beautiful horse named *Foxhunter* to a famous victory. They were an invincible pairing; winning 78 international trophies together during the 1950s. After his death, in 1959, *Foxhunter* was buried on top of the Blorenge, where you'll see a small memorial plaque. Sir Harry, who was born in Aberdare but actually lived near Abergavenny, died after a long illness in 1999, aged 88. His ashes were scattered by the grave of his famous mount.

summit was once marked with an ancient burial cairn, which is where all the stones come from. From here, keep heading in the same direction, now aiming towards the

two huge masts that you can see on the horizon. Shortly before you reach the masts, you'll see a car park ahead. Approximately 50 yds (46m) before you reach this, you'll see a faint grassy track that leads off diagonally right, towards a seat. Follow this and then clamber over the small bank to find the grave of *Foxhunter*, a famous horse which was buried here **C**.

How old was **Foxhunter** *when he died?*

Now follow the path out to the car park and masts, where you need to turn left to walk down the narrow lane to the car park.

Quarried limestone, the Blorenge

Craig Cerrig-gleisiad

This walk is two walks in one. The longer outing circumnavigates the dramatic escarpment of Craig Cerrig-gleisiad on easy-to-follow paths but it involves a very steep descent, which may not be suitable for all the family. The shorter walk takes an easy trail into the very heart of the National Nature Reserve and offers a chance to see the geological effects of the receding Ice Ages as well as the unique flora and fauna left behind.

START Craig Cerrig-gleisiad picnic area
(grid ref: SN 971222)
DISTANCE 4 miles (6.4km)
or 1.2 miles (1.9km)
TIME 2½ hours or 1 hour
PARKING At the picnic area
ROUTE FEATURES Rocky escarpment and cliffs; steep climb; clear tracks; muddy paths; stream crossings. *Shorter route: rocky escarpment and cliffs; muddy paths; some stiles*

12

From the lay-by, go through the kissing-gate and follow the footpath up the valley for 300 yds (274m) to a dry stone wall **A**. Go through the gap in the wall and turn right to follow the clear path around the hillside with the wall to your right. Drop to cross a small brook and climb slightly to continue in the same direction with great views over the Tarell Valley to the high mountains of the Brecon Beacons on the other side of the A470. Cross another brook and

Craig Cerrig-gleisiad from Fan Fawr

PUBLIC TRANSPORT Summer bus service from Brecon and Merthyr Tydfil
REFRESHMENTS None
PUBLIC TOILETS None
PICNIC/PLAY AREA Picnic area at the start
ORDNANCE SURVEY MAPS Explorer OL12 (Brecon Beacons Western & Central areas), Landranger 160 (Brecon Beacons)

climb back up again. Now continue until you reach a stile that leads onto a clear track, with fine views to the north **B**.

Turn left and climb steeply up the hill, all the time staying on the clear main track. Eventually you'll come to a gate and a stile, that give access to open ground beyond. Continue along the track until a clear turning to the right leads you to the trig point that marks the summit of Fan Frynch **C**.

Facing back the way that you came, you'll see two tracks leading away from the trig point. Take the right-hand one and ignore a fork to the right almost immediately. Continue to another fork and bear right to drop back onto the main track **D**. Turn right onto this and follow the fence along until you spot a stile on your left. Cross this and turn right, to follow the fence along, now on your right. The path drops slightly and then climbs steeply to the top of Craig Cerrig-gleisiad **E**; which is

> **?** *How many different flowers and birds can you spot?*

Craig Cerrig-gleisiad in snow

coincidentally the same height as Fan Frynych.

Now follow the path above the steep cliffs and down to the left, where it drops very steeply back into the valley below. *The ground is very steep here so great care is needed.* Stay with the main path and it will lead you to the stream that you followed on the way up. Cross this and turn right to walk back through the hole in the wall and down to the lay-by and picnic area.

For the shorter route, from **Ⓐ**, *keep straight ahead and walk in towards the foot of the cliffs. You can walk to the very base of the steeper ground if you wish. The area here makes for interesting*

exploration so take your time and enjoy the unusual nature and magnificent scenery. Return by the same route. ●

The **north-facing cliffs** of Craig Cerrig-gleisiad – which translates to Blue-stone Rock – were **formed** by glacial action **during the last Ice Age**. The ice scoured out the deep hollow in the hillside, that you see today, before depositing the rocks it picked up into large banks known as '**moraine**'. Amazingly, the cool conditions created by the constant shade of the north-facing cliffs, have enabled a selection of arctic – alpine plants to continue to flourish. These plants, which include saxifrages and roseroot, thrive on the lime-rich soil around the cliffs. The diversity of the National Nature Reserve stretches beyond flora with 16 different species of butterfly and over 80 species of bird observed here too.

13 *Grwyne Fawr Reservoir*

START Mynydd Du Forest (grid ref: SO 252284)

DISTANCE 4 miles (6.4km)

TIME 2 hours

PARKING At the start

ROUTE FEATURES Clear rocky paths; grassy meadows; open moorland; reservoir; riverside road; picnic areas

The Grwyne Fawr Valley runs all the way from the highest ground in the Black Mountains to the village of Glangrwyney, near Abergavenny, where it finally empties into the Usk. The hillsides that form the head of the valley cradle a sizeable reservoir that makes a fine objective for a walk. This is a lengthy but easy expedition ending with a beautiful riverside stroll.

Head out of the far end of the car park and turn right onto the road. After just a few paces, bear right onto a steep stony track and climb up with the wood to your right and the valley floor below you to the left. The woodland is a great place to spot different fungi; especially in autumn and early winter. Continue up, eventually leaving the woods behind **A** and crossing open moorland, still with the ever deepening valley down to your left. The steep hillside on the other side of the valley forms the lower flanks of the Gadair Ridge and is topped with Waun Fach and Pen y Gadair Fawr, the two highest peaks in the Black Mountains.

Continue through a succession of gates until the track eventually levels and you see a stand of conifers ahead. This marks the reservoir grounds. Continue until you reach the grounds and go through the gate on your left to gain access to the huge dam **B**. Walk across the dam and then, when you get to the other side,

PUBLIC TRANSPORT None

REFRESHMENTS None

PUBLIC TOILETS None

PICNIC/PLAY AREA Picnic areas at and near the start

ORDNANCE SURVEY MAPS Explorer OL13 (Brecon Beacons Eastern area), Landranger 161 (The Black Mountains)

turn left to climb a steep bank dotted with a few trees. Continue in the same direction until you reach the far side of the bank, where you'll see a clearer path leading down to a fence.

Drop to the fence and bear left to follow it down to a stile. Cross this

The Grwyne Fawr Reservoir was once the highest reservoir in the whole of Britain, with the upper water level reaching an impressive 1,935ft (590m) above sea level. Work began on the **dam** as early as 1912 but the hostilities of the First World War delayed the proceedings and it **wasn't completed until 1928**. The dam spans some 327m and the walls at its base are over 40m thick. When full the reservoir can hold around 370 million gallons of water, which is then carried to towns as far away as Abertillery by a network of underground pipes. The reservoir's biggest claim to fame was when Prince Harry was photographed abseiling down the dam wall as part of an adventure weekend in 1998.

and drop down the steep hillside on a faint path that eventually leads out onto a narrow tarmac lane **C**, which is the dam access road. Turn right onto this and continue easily along it with the Grwyne Fawr River on your left. There are numerous rapids and cascades all the way down and this is a great spot to see dippers; small black and white birds that feed on aquatic larvae by actually walking beneath the fast flowing water.

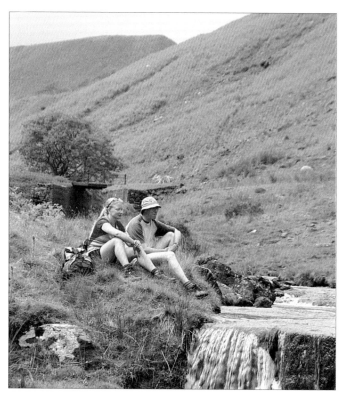

Grwyne Fawr, Brecon Beacons

Herons also ply their trade on the banks of the river.

Follow the road down, bridging the river after a short distance, and then passing beneath an isolated

> ? *How wide do you think the dam wall is at the top — on the part that you walk over?*

cottage. Eventually you'll reach a lovely level grassy area that separates you from the riverbanks. This is a fine picnic spot but be warned; it gets very busy in the summer. Keep as close to the banks as you can and continue easily downstream until you pass the track you followed on the way out. Continue for a few paces and then turn left, back into the car park. ●

Goytre Wharf and Pentre Hill

START Goytre Wharf (grid ref: SO 312063)

DISTANCE 4½ miles (7.2km)

TIME 2 hours

PARKING Pay and Display at the start

ROUTE FEATURES Woodland trails; muddy field paths; meadows; canal towpath

14

Goytre Wharf is the undisputed highlight of a narrow finger of land that defines the south east corner of the National Park. This is an enjoyable ramble, which starts and finishes on the waterside, but climbs steeply up into the surrounding woodland, where it offers great views over the Monmouthshire countryside. A short detour can be made to an excellent, tucked-away, country inn; or there's a great restaurant back at the canal side.

✎ From the car park, head back out of the drive to the road and turn left. Immediately turn right, over a stile, and walk up through

Originally known as the Breckneck and Abergavenny Canal, the 33-mile long **Brecon and Monmouthshire Canal** was constructed between 1797 and 1812, to link Brecon with the Bristol Channel port of Newport. It was mainly used to carry stone and processed lime from local quarries but these days it sees only leisure traffic.

the field to another stile. Keep ahead again to another stile and now keep the hedge to your left to continue uphill to yet another stile at the foot of some woodland Ⓐ. Cross the stile and turn right, to walk along a broad forest track that skirts the bottom of the woodland. Ignore a track leading up into the wood and continue around until you reach a junction with another track that drops down to your right. If you miss it, you'll soon

PUBLIC TRANSPORT Buses between Abergavenny and Goytre village
REFRESHMENTS Restaurant at the start and the Goose and Cuckoo public house a few minutes from the walk
PUBLIC TOILETS At start
PICNIC/PLAY AREA Both at the start
ORDNANCE SURVEY MAPS Explorer OL13 (Brecon Beacons Eastern area), Landranger 161 (The Black Mountains)

Canal boat near Goytre Wharf

Which trees that you see on the walk will produce acorns?

come to a gate that blocks your way. Drop down to the road **B**.

Now cross the road to walk up the narrow lane opposite. Continue past a drive on the right, that leads to a large house, and you'll soon come to the corner of a wood on your right; with footpaths going both right and left. Take the left one, and climb steeply up the edge of a field and through a gap to continue up the edge of the next field. At the top of this one, bear right to walk around the top of the field to a gateway. Go through this and keep to the right-hand edge of the next field to a waymarker and a stile beneath a house **C**.

Turn right here and walk along the top of a field to a stile that leads onto a sunken track. Turn right onto this track and follow it all the way down to the road . Turn left and immediately right, to drop down to a bridge. *For the Goose and Cuckoo, ignore the right turn and continue uphill.* Cross the bridge before turning right onto a waymarked footpath. The path is vague at this point but keep ahead for approximately 10 yds (9m) and then bear left to climb steeply up a bank to join a good drive at the top. Bear right onto this and follow it past a house, keeping the house to your left.

Now keep straight ahead until you reach a wood. Go over the stile and turn right and then left to walk around a fence, with a pond to your right. Continue to a stile that leads back onto open pasture and bear half right to drop to the right-hand hedge. Now follow the field edge down to a stile, where you keep straight ahead again, to walk along with the hedge now to your right. Continue until you are almost back on the canal, where a waymark post directs you left, across the field to a gate. Go through this and follow the track along to an open area, where you turn right to cross the canal on a bridge. Drop down to join the towpath and follow it all the way back to Goytre Wharf. Here, you bear left to drop down from the towpath and then turn right to walk beneath the aqueduct back to the car park.

Brecon and Monmouthshire Canal near Goytre

15 The Taf Fechan Forest

START Owl's Grove recreation area (grid ref: SO 048162)
DISTANCE 4 miles (6.4km)
TIME 2 hours
PARKING At the start
ROUTE FEATURES Woodland; riverside paths; boggy moorland

Delightfully easy walking around a picturesque valley that cuts deeply into the southern slopes of the National Park's highest mountains. This walk has a little of everything from broad forest tracks, with fine views, to a secret winding riverside path that feels almost enchanted. Some sections can be wet and muddy so good boots will be an advantage.

Owl Grove shelter, Taf Fechan Forest

Walk out onto the road and turn right to walk steeply uphill for a few minutes. As you reach the top, bear left onto a broad forest track **A** and then, after just a few paces, keep straight ahead at a fork, with another track dropping to your left. Continue along here for ½ mile (800m) or so and keep left at a fork, through a gate, to continue easily, with fine views over the valley below, to a junction with a narrow lane **B**.

PUBLIC TRANSPORT Summer bus service from Brecon and Talybont-on-Usk
REFRESHMENTS None
PUBLIC TOILETS None
PICNIC/PLAY AREA At the start
ORDNANCE SURVEY MAPS Explorer OL12 (Brecon Beacons Western & Central areas), Landranger 160 (Brecon Beacons)

Afon Taf Fechan, Taf Fechan Forest

Turn right onto the lane and then turn straightaway right again, onto a broad muddy track that climbs up the edge of the forest. Follow this uphill, now with excellent views across the head of the Taf Fechan Valley, until you reach a gate above a deep, steep-sided ravine **C**. Do not go through the gate, instead, turn left over a stile and walk downhill, on a grassy path, keeping the ravine down to your right. Follow the fence down and as it bears left at the bottom, follow it around to a stile directly ahead.

Cross the stile and turn right to drop over a narrow grassy strip to the waterworks access road **D**, where there will probably be a lot of cars parked.

Now turn right through a small gate, into the waterworks, and keep ahead and slightly left to pick up a clear path. Drop down into a dip and cross a concrete bridge over the reservoir outfall before climbing steeply up onto the grassy top of the dam. Bear left here to follow this along, with great views up the valley to Pen y Fan and Corn Du, the highest mountains in the National Park, and then keep straight ahead to go through a gate and out onto open moorland **E**

Bear left to follow a faint path downhill (waymark on post). Merge with another path and keep right to drop down over a brook. Now aim for the stile that you see ahead and this marks the start of a clear but often boggy and muddy

The **two Neuadd reservoirs** passed on the walk were constructed to supply water to Merthyr Tydfil during its heyday as a boomtown in the industrial revolution. The lower one was opened in 1884 but demand soon outstripped supply and the river was flooded again, higher up the valley.

path that heads down the valley with the forest to your right and the Taf Fechan River down to your left. The path gradually improves

The Brecon Beacons from Neuadd Reservoir

to become
a well-surfaced
forest track after ½
mile (800m) or so. Stay
with it, keeping ahead the
whole time, and eventually
you'll meet the road **F**.

Turn left onto the road and walk
uphill to a bridge with spectacular
waterfalls to your left. Cross the
bridge and turn right, as if entering
the car park, and then turn right
again, to follow a good path into
the woods with the river to your
right. Follow this easily along,

> **?** *Which is the tallest of the three mountains that you can see at the head of the valley?*

passing a wooden footbridge to the
right after a few paces. Continue
along the bank until, after
approximately ½ mile (800m), the
path veers left away from the river,
now following the bank of a
smaller tributary. Continue easily
upstream to a small footbridge on
the right. Cross this and you'll see
the car park straight ahead. ●

16 The Waterfalls Walk

START Porth yr Ogof car park
(grid ref: SN 928124)
DISTANCE 5 miles (8km)
TIME 2½ hours
PARKING Supervised fee-paying car park at the start
ROUTE FEATURES Slippery rock; roots; steep steps; muddy tracks; forest trails; waterfalls

The Ystradfellte waterfalls are one of the real jewels in the Brecon Beacons crown; especially when the cloud comes down, obscuring the views from the hilltops. This is a longish walk, and there are a few very steep stepped sections to negotiate along the way. The rewards are wonderful though with some quite breathtaking scenery in places. Take waterproofs if you wish to walk behind the falls.

Before heading off for the waterfalls, it's well worth visiting Porth yr Ogof, one of the largest cave entrances in Wales, which is situated just a few metres below the car park. Descend the steps that lead from the bottom of the car park, beneath the toilet block, and then turn left at the bottom to walk along the rocky bank to the gargantuan mouth of the cave. *It's possible to walk a short way in but great care is needed, as the rock can* *be very slippery and the river is very powerful and dangerous.*

Walk back up towards the car park and bear right to walk out to the road Ⓐ.

Go straight across to cross a stile and follow the footpath down into a dip (cave entrance) and back up again. Keep ahead, with the fence to your left and trees to your right, until you drop down onto a broad

PUBLIC TRANSPORT None
REFRESHMENTS None
PUBLIC TOILETS At the start
PICNIC/PLAY AREA At the start
ORDNANCE SURVEY MAPS Explorer OL12 (Brecon Beacons Western & Central areas), Landranger 160 (Brecon Beacons)

The **geology** of this area is fairly complex with layers of carboniferous limestone interspersed with layers of much harder old red sandstone as well as considerably softer shales. The **waterfalls** have been formed where layers of the harder rock have created shelves that cannot be worn down by the fast flowing rivers. As soon as the water passes downstream of these shelves, it continues the erosion process, creating a steep drop.

grassy riverbank. Bear left here and follow the Afon Mellte downstream. *The path is easy in some places but awkward in others. Take care crossing the steeper sections and remember that the rocks and roots can be slippery.* Like many of the rivers in the area, this is a good place to see dippers and some of the slower moving pools are also home to kingfishers. Eventually you'll come to a footbridge that spans the river **B**.

Do not cross the bridge, instead keep ahead to drop into a dip and climb steeply out again. Continue up to a fence on your left and then, where you see a wooden fence ahead and to the right, climb up a few more feet to

There are four big waterfalls on this walk but how many smaller ones can you count?

join a good broad forest track. Continue in the same direction to start with and then follow it as it curves round to the left. Keep the small brook down to your right and the tightly knit conifers to your left to walk to a crossroads of tracks **C**.

Bear right here, which is signposted Sgwd yr Eira, and follow the red-topped waymarks along the forest track. Stay with this for a while now, ducking into a particularly dark section of woodland before it opens out into mixed woodland again. Continue until a waymark post directs you right, downhill. Drop down a few steps and continue down until you join into an open track, that runs along the edge of the steep gorge ahead **D**.

Turn right onto this, and then turn left, down some steep steps, to the Afon

Hepste below. Turn left to walk to the waterfall, which is known as Sgwd yr Eira (the Falls of Snow). It is possible to walk behind the waterfall if you wish but you may want to wear waterproofs, as it does get very wet. *Also, watch your footing – it's very slippery.*

Now climb back up the steps to the top path and turn left. Continue

Sgwd yr Eira

Sgwd Isaf Clun Gwyn, Ystradfellte

easily along here, passing a seat on your left, and you'll eventually see a green waymark directing you downhill to the left **E**. Follow this down and keep left at a fork. This will lead you to Sgwd y Pannwr (the Falls of the Fuller) **F**. Now follow the Afon Mellte upstream past a number of pools to the next waterfall, which is Sgwd Isaf Clun-Gwyn (the Lower Falls of the White Meadow) **G**. For the best views, scramble up the bank for a few metres.

Now retrace your steps back downstream and bear left at the first opportunity to climb back up to the fork you visited earlier. Keep ahead to climb back up to the top path again **E**. Bear left onto this

and follow it for some distance now, until you see a wooden fence down to your left. This marks the viewing position above the final waterfall, Sgwd Uchaf Clun-Gwyn (the Upper Falls of the White Meadow) **H**. Drop to the left for the viewing area.

Climb back up to the path above and turn left to follow the fence along to meet the path that you walked along earlier. Keep left to follow this down to the footbridge you passed on the way out and keep ahead to follow the Afon Mellte back upstream. The grassy bank near the car park makes a great place to while away the rest of the afternoon if you've time to spare.

17 *The Sugar Loaf*

START Mynydd Llanwenarth viewpoint (grid ref: SO 268167)

DISTANCE 4½ miles (7.2km)

TIME 3 hours

PARKING At the start

ROUTE FEATURES Grassy mountain paths; rocky summit

This is one of the toughest walks in the book but still perfectly achievable if taken slowly and steadily. The Sugar Loaf stands aloof from the Black Mountains but offers wonderful views across them, as well as over the Usk Valley and the town of Abergavenny. Meadow pipits, skylarks and even the occasional grouse live on the heathery slopes, and ravens frequent the rocky tops.

Standing in the car park and looking up the slope, there are three obvious tracks leading away.

The lowest, to your left, is a tarmac drive. The highest goes straight uphill past a National Trust sign. Between these, running diagonally half-left is a broad grassy track, dotted with a few rocks. Take this and follow it upwards to the corner of a dry stone wall **A**. Keep straight ahead, with the wall to your left, and ignore any tracks that lead off to the right.

Eventually, you'll start to drop into a deep valley, where the path finally veers away from the wall and drops diagonally across the hillside towards the far corner of a wood. Upon reaching the corner of the wood, turn left to descend a steep grassy path to the stream **B**. Keep ahead to climb away from the stream, and follow the obvious main path steeply uphill and onto a distinct shoulder, with a steep slope to your right and a wall to your left. Continue until the path reaches the crest and then,

PUBLIC TRANSPORT None

REFRESHMENTS None

PUBLIC TOILETS None

ORDNANCE SURVEY MAPS Explorer OL13 (Brecon Beacons Eastern area), Landranger 161 (The Black Mountains)

with the corner of the wall and a gate directly ahead of you **C**, turn right to cross some rough ground. You will locate a good path that climbs up the centre of the grassy ridge with good views in both directions.

As the track levels, you'll be joined by another track coming in from the left. Ignore this and continue straight ahead to climb steeply up the narrowing ridge. This is a great place to spot birds with meadow pipits and skylarks a very common sight. You'll probably hear the incessant chattering call of the skylark long before you see it so keep your eyes open above you to see if you can see one hovering in the sky. As you get higher, and the bilberry and bracken give way to heather, you may also see or hear the odd red grouse.

Looking towards the Sugar Loaf from Abergavenny

A final steep section gives access to jumbled rocks that mark the western end of the summit. The rocks offer wonderful views west, across the Grwyne Fawr Valley to the Black Mountains. Continue straight ahead, on a narrow path that weaves between the rocks, and you'll soon come to the whitewashed trig point **D**. It's a good idea to take a few moments to gain your bearings here. Look back down towards the car park, which you cannot actually see from the summit, and you'll notice that there are a lot of different tracks that cross the hillside; many of them not shown on the map. The valley down to your left is St Mary's Vale (see Walk 3). The descent route contours around the head of this valley rather than dropping into it. Follow the narrow path that leads downhill to the right from the trig

The Brecon Beacons from Neuadd Reservoir

point and continue steeply down until you reach the level ground that marks the head of St Mary's Vale. Circle around the valley and

Can you recognise the other two Abergavenny mountains of the Blorenge and Ysgyryd Fawr?

The **Sugar Loaf**, or Mynydd Pen-y-fâl, to give it its true Welsh name, is one of the most distinctive and popular peaks in the National Park. Its rugged cone-shaped summit can be seen from many miles around and its bracken-covered slopes are criss-crossed with a good network of grassy paths that make it one of the easier peaks to climb. It's quite distinct from the Black Mountains, which sit on the other side of the gaping chasm of the Grwyne Fawr Valley (see Walk 13), and is usually classified as **one of the three Abergavenny Peaks, along with Ysgyryd Fawr and the Blorenge** (see Walk 11).

continue along the main track, with the valley now to your left and the crest of the ridge to your right, until you reach a broad grassy square that is actually a fairly major crossroads of tracks. Turn right here to cross the crest of the ridge and you should be able to see a wall ahead – this is the wall that you followed on the way out. Continue until you reach it and then bear left to retrace your earlier footsteps back to the car park.

18 *The Cat's Back and Black Hill*

START Black Hill picnic area (grid ref: SO 288327)
DISTANCE 5 miles (8km)
TIME 3 hours
PARKING At the start
ROUTE FEATURES Rocky ridge; open moorland; steep valley path; narrow lane

A pedigree mountain walk that should not prove too much of a challenge as long as it's taken slowly and the weather stays fine. The rewards for the effort are tremendous; with an airy traverse of one of the Black Mountain's finest ridges and some stunning views over the Hereford countryside to the Malvern Hills.

Leave the car park and picnic tables and head uphill towards the obvious hillside. Cross the rickety old stile (or go through the gate) to gain access to the open hillside. The main track bears away to the right to contour around the hillside so leave it to the left and climb steeply up the centre of the obvious sharp prow. This is the steepest section of the walk and, in fact, one of the steepest paths in the whole book. It's not very long though, so take your time and you'll soon be cresting the rise at the southern end of a wonderful narrow ridge Ⓐ.

Once up, keep ahead to follow the airy skyline walkway easily northwards over numerous short and craggy steps. The views to the east, over the flat lands of the Herefordshire countryside, are wonderful. So are those to the west, across the magnificent Olchon Valley to the Hatterrall Ridge, which actually defines the

PUBLIC TRANSPORT None suitable
REFRESHMENTS None
PUBLIC TOILETS None
PICNIC/PLAY AREA At the start
ORDNANCE SURVEY MAPS Explorer OL13 (Brecon Beacons Eastern area), Landranger 161 (The Black Mountains)

The Cat's Back, Black Hill

border between England and Wales as well as forming the eastern boundary of the National Park. You'll also notice some spectacular thorn trees growing out of the near vertical valley sides.

Eventually the spur starts to broaden and you'll start the final easy ascent to Black Hill's 2,100ft (640m) trig point **B**, which you'll see protruding sharply from the heather and bilberry. Once there, follow the faint path away from the summit and pass close to a small pond before continuing easily

upwards. Continue for approximately 15 minutes until you see a small cairn that marks a barely discernable junction of paths **C**. Turn left here, onto a very faint grassy track, and follow it down into an obvious notch that quickly deepens to become the head of the spectacular Olchon Valley.

Technically speaking this walk is neither in the Brecon Beacons National Park or, in fact, in Wales, but it is **one of the finest rambles in the Black Mountains** and it would be remiss to leave it out.

Stay with the path as it becomes more established; dropping down the side of a small brook and eventually developing into a broad and rocky track that dips steeply down the head of the valley, where you'll see some small waterfalls decorating the Olchon Brook to your right and some lofty crags crowning the steep hillside opposite. Continue steeply down until the going eases and the path flattens out nicely to make a

The Black Mountains from the Cat's Back

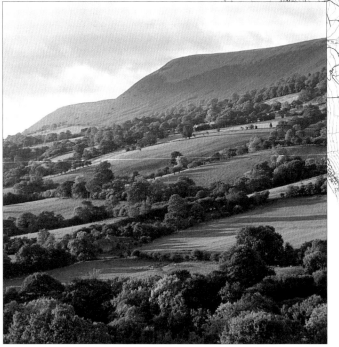

pleasant and gentle walk, a few metres above the infant river.

Continue over a couple of small tributaries to a gate in a corner that leads in turn onto a sunken green lane. Follow this easily down until it merges with a narrow tarmac road **D**. Bear left onto this lane and follow it for nearly one mile (1.6km) to a T-junction. Turn left here and climb steeply back up to the car park on the same lane that you drove in on earlier. ●

The highest ground in England is actually Scafell Pike in the Lake District, which is 3,205ft (977m) above sea level. There is often debate about which is the highest ground in southern England, an accolade often incorrectly handed to High Willhays on Dartmoor, which is actually only 2,037ft (621m) above sea level as opposed to the **highest point of the Hatterrall Ridge**, very close to this walk, which **is 2,306ft (703m)**. Even Black Hill, which is actually visited on this walk, is notably higher than any of the ground on Dartmoor or Derbyshire's Peak District.

This walk is very close to the border of England and Wales. Which country is Herefordshire part of?

19 *The Usk Reservoir*

START Car park and picnic area near Pont'ar Wysg (grid ref: SN 819271)
DISTANCE 5½ miles (8.8km)
TIME 2½ hours
PARKING At the start
ROUTE FEATURES Forest tracks; lakeside paths; tarmac lane

This is the longest walk in the book but it follows good trails and is therefore reasonably easy-going. The reservoir itself is a hidden gem. Concealed by dense woodland and surrounded by some very remote moorland it offers great views over the surrounding countryside and is also a good place to spot wildlife, particularly waterfowl and red kites.

From the car park, walk back out onto the road and cross it to go through a gate onto a path. You'll see the bicycle trail waymark disc on the gatepost and will be following these all the way round. Keep ahead, ignoring a couple of tracks that come in from the right, and then climb briefly before swinging round to the left. Continue past a wide turning area and drop down to cross a footbridge that actually spans the infant River Usk **A**.

> This walk actually follows the **family cycle trail** around the reservoir. Keep your eyes open for the waymark posts that will make navigation easy for you.

Climb away from this and continue along what is the most undulating section of the whole walk. You'll soon start to get some

PUBLIC TRANSPORT None
REFRESHMENTS None
PUBLIC TOILETS None
PICNIC/PLAY AREA There are picnic areas all the way around the reservoir and at the start
ORDNANCE SURVEY MAPS Explorer OL12 (Brecon Beacons Western & Central areas), Landranger 160 (Brecon Beacons)

views of the water down through the trees to your right and eventually you'll swing round to the right and drop down to the

> **How many different types of duck can you see on the water?**

water level, with some fairly bleak looking moorland to your left **B**. There's also a picnic table here, if you fancy stopping a while.

Cross the footbridge and continue uphill until the track turns a sharp right to start heading along the northern shore. This is a lovely

Usk Reservoir

section, with the water below you to the right and some rather grand Caledonian pines scattered along the trail. Keep ahead, with great views over the lake, until another waymark finally directs you left, away from the water and uphill slightly **C**.

You'll pass a grassy track coming in from the left but keep on the main cycle trail and you'll shortly reach another junction, where you bear round to the right, to run parallel with the shores once again. Stay with this and you'll cross a small tributary before dropping slowly back to water level close to the ornate building that protrudes into the waters. Keep ahead and go

The **River Usk** rises up from a boggy moorland plateau just a few miles south of the reservoir, in the shadow of the magnificent mountains of the Carmarthen Fan. It drops easily from the bleak moorland to the reservoir forming the boundary between Powys and Carmarthenshire as it goes. From here, the river gains steam again, plummeting over the dam before continuing east past Sennybridge and on to Brecon, where it meanders southwards to divide the Brecon Beacons from the Black Mountains. At Llangynidr it swings east again, running almost parallel with the Brecon and Monmouthshire Canal. This lovely stretch ends at Abergavenny where the Usk is joined by the Gavenny River (see Walk 2). Here, it bears south east and continues over much flatter ground to join the Bristol Channel at Newport.

through a barrier to join the tarmac drive and then follow this around to the left and then right, to round the northern tip of the reservoir **D**.

The drive now cruises along the shore, with a few picnic tables to your right. Pass beneath a large house on your left and continue to the end of the dam, where you'll see a few small boats moored. Turn right to cross the dam and keep ahead at the other end to walk through the car park and up the road. This section follows the narrow lane for a few minutes but *whilst you should obviously take care, it doesn't see much traffic.*

Bear round to the left, ignoring an

> The **Usk Reservoir** lies at just over 1,000ft (305m) above sea level and is the most recent of the Brecon Beacons' reservoirs opening as recently as 1955.

obvious forest track to your right, and climb slightly to another track on the right, this one marked with the cycle trail signing **E**. Turn right here and keep ahead at a crossroads of tracks to another, where you should turn left, uphill slightly. Follow this for around 300 yds (274m) where it starts to curve round to the right. Stay with it as it drops easily to join another track at the bottom. This is the track that you started on. Turn left onto this and follow it back to the gate and across the road to the car park. ●

Usk Reservoir from the dam

20 *Pen y Fan*

START Storey Arms
(grid ref: SN 982203)
DISTANCE 5 miles (8km)
TIME 3 hours
PARKING At the start
ROUTE FEATURES Rocky
paths; steep climbs;
mountain summits

This is the toughest walk in the book, as you'd probably expect from the highest mountain in the National Park. The good news is that it's probably not as tough as you'd expect starting quite high in the first place and following clear paths all the way. The rewards are incredible with views that really do match the satisfaction of the achievement.

Cross the road and hop over the stile, next to the telephone box, outside the Storey Arms Outdoor Adventure Centre.

Now follow a clear path up the hillside, leaving the plantation behind and crossing the open moorland that makes up the

southern flanks of Y Gyrn – the bare rounded summit over to your left.

> Pen y Fan is usually climbed in a linear, out and back fashion, using the main track used here in descent. The **circular route** described here is a lot more interesting yet not much more difficult.

PUBLIC TRANSPORT Buses between Brecon and Merthyr Tydfil
REFRESHMENTS There's often a snack van in the car park
PUBLIC TOILETS In the car park near the start
ORDNANCE SURVEY MAPS Explorer OL12 (Brecon Beacons Western & Central areas), Landranger 160 (Brecon Beacons)

You'll soon gain a broad ridge, where you need to cross a stile and drop down to the very infant Taf Fawr River **A**. The way ahead is obvious now, with a rough and badly eroded track heading directly up the hillside on the other side of the valley. Follow it until it reaches the steep escarpment edge high above the deeply gouged valley of Cwm Llwch **B**. Far below you'll see the small lake of Llyn y Cwm

Falls on Storey Arms Path

Llwch and towering above this, you'll see the steep crags of Corn Du.

If you've got the energy, bear left here and drop down the obvious path for about 300 yds (274m), where you'll find the Tommy Jones memorial. Remember that you have to climb back up to this spot afterwards. If you'd rather save your energy, bear right and climb the obvious path steeply up to the rocky ramparts that guard the summit of Corn Du. The table-topped summit is crowned with a sprawling cairn **C**.

The way to Pen y Fan is straightforward now. Drop easily

? What date did they finally find Tommy Jones?

into the shallow notch that separates the two peaks and then climb up onto the highest point in southern Britain. Whilst the summit is flat and, at first glance, not all that exciting, walk over to the precipitous north east face and you'll start to get an idea of the scale and grandeur of this beautiful mountain **D**.

To descend, walk back across towards Corn Du and then bear left to follow the obvious track that contours around the summit into the pass on the other side, which is

Pen y Fan

Tommy Jones was a five-year-old miner's son. In August 1900, he visited the area with his father to see his grandfather, who lived on a farm below the peaks. They walked from the old railway station in Brecon and stopped for a rest at a local army camp, where they were met by his grandfather and also his 13-year-old cousin, Willie. The two older men were enjoying the company of the soldiers so decided to stay at the camp for a while. They sent the two boys on ahead to tell Tommy's grandmother of their impending arrival. It was getting quite late and, as it started to get dark, Tommy was scared and decided to return to his father. Willie continued to the farm to tell his grandmother as arranged. Tragically however, Tommy never made it back to the camp.

A huge search ensued. The army became involved and so did the daily newspapers – one actually offering a reward for information. Sadly, weeks went by without any sight of him and then, a local woman dreamed of the boy and led her husband straight up onto a ridge, where she'd never been before, and where they discovered the small boy's body. He had died of exhaustion and exposure. An **obelisk** now stands close to the spot where his body was found. It was moved a few years ago to reduce erosion.

known as Bwlch Duwynt **E**. This is a major junction of paths and you need to take the obvious right-hand one that descends steeply down the hillside towards the

Tommy Jones obelisk

A470. Some sections of this have been man-made out of local sandstone to reduce erosion, which is a big problem in these hills.

Follow the track easily down for just over a mile and you'll see the Taf Fawr River down to your right. Continue to a ford **F** and go through the kissing-gate into the main car park. Turn right into the car park and follow it to its far end where a gravel footpath (signposted Taff Trail) takes over. Continue along the side of the plantation, with the road on your left, and then cross the road to return to the start. ●

Further Information

Safety on the Hills

The hills, mountains and moorlands of Britain, though of modest height compared with those in many other countries, need to be treated with respect. Friendly and inviting in good weather, they can quickly be transformed into wet, misty, windswept and potentially dangerous areas of wilderness in bad weather. Even on an out-wardly fine and settled summer day, conditions can rapidly deteriorate. In winter, of course, the weather can be even more erratic and the hours of daylight are much shorter.

Therefore it is advisable to always take both warm and waterproof clothing, sufficient nourishing food, a hot drink, first-aid kit, torch and whistle. Wear suitable footwear, such as strong walking boots or shoes that give a good grip over rocky terrain and on slippery slopes. Try to obtain a local weather forecast and bear it in mind before you start. Do not be afraid to abandon your proposed route and return to your starting point in the event of a sudden and unexpected deterioration in the weather. Do not go alone. Allow enough time to finish the walk well before nightfall.

Forest track and trees, Coed Taf Fawr, Garwnant

Brecon and Monmouthshire Canal, Gilwern

Most of the walks described in this book do not venture into remote wilderness areas and will be safe to do, given due care and respect, at any time of year in all but the most unreasonable weather. Indeed, a crisp, fine winter day often provides perfect walking conditions, with firm ground underfoot and a clarity that is not possible to achieve in the other seasons of the year. A few walks, however, are suitable only for reasonably fit and experienced hill walkers able to use a compass and should definitely not be tackled by anyone else during the winter months or in bad weather, especially high winds and mist. These are indicated in the general description that precedes each of the walks.

Follow the Country Code

- Enjoy the countryside and respect its life and work
- Guard against all risk of fire
- Take your litter home
- Fasten all gates
- Help to keep all water clean
- Keep your dogs under control
- Protect wildlife, plants and trees
- Keep to public paths across farmland
- Take special care on country roads
- Leave livestock, crops and machinery alone
- Make no unnecessary noise
- Use gates and stiles to cross fences, hedges and walls

(The Countryside Agency)

Brecon Beacons National Park Authority
Plas y Ffynnon, Cambrian Way, Brecon, Powys LD3 7HP
Tel. 01874 624437
www.breconbeacons.org

CADW Welsh Historic Monuments
National Assembly for Wales, Cathays Park, Cardiff CF10 3NQ
Tel. 029 2050 0200
www.cadw.wales.gov.uk

Campaign for the Protection of Rural Wales
Ty Gwyn, 31 High Street Welshpool, Powys SY21 7YD
Tel. 01938 552525
www.cprw.org.uk

Coed Cymru
The Old Sawmill, Tregynon Newtown, Powys SY16 3PL
Tel. 01686 650777
www.coedcymru.org.uk

Countryside Council for Wales
Maes-y-Ffynnon, Penrhosgarnedd Bangor, Gwynedd LL57 2DW
Tel. 08451 306229
www.ccw.gov.uk

National Trust Office for Wales
Trinity Square, Llandudno LL30 2DE
Tel. 01492 860123
www.nationaltrust.org.uk

Ordnance Survey
Romsey Road, Maybush, Southampton
SO16 4GU
Tel. 08456 05 05 05 (Lo-call)
www.ordnancesurvey.co.uk

Ramblers' Association
2nd Floor, Camelford House, 87-90 Albert Embankment, London SE1 7TW
Tel. 020 7339 8500
www.ramblers.org.uk

Ramblers' Association Wales
1 Cathedral Road, Cardiff CF11 9HA
Tel. 029 2064 7565
www.ramblers.org.uk/wales

Youth Hostel Association (England and Wales)
Trevelyan House, 8 St Stephens Hill, St Albans, Herts AL1 2DY
Tel. 0870 870 8808
www.yha.org.uk

Wildlife Trusts in and around the Brecon Beacons:
Brecknock Wildlife Trust
Lion House, Bethel Square Brecon, Powys LD3 7AY

Tel. 01874 625708
www.wildlifetrust.org.uk/brecknock

Gwent Wildlife Trust
Seddon House, Dingestow
Monmouth NP25 4DY
Tel. 01600 740358
www.wildlifetrust.org.uk/gwent

The Wildlife Trust of South and West Wales
The Nature Centre, Fountain Road
Tondu, Bridgend CF32 0EH
Tel. 01656 724100
www.wildlifetrust.org.uk/wtsww

Tourist Information Centres:
Brecon Tourist Information Office
Cattle Market Car Park
Brecon LD3 9DA
Tel. 01874 622485

Other tourist information centres:
Abergavenny
Tel. 01873 857588

Crickhowell
Tel. 01873 812105

Hay-on-Wye
Tel. 01497 820144

Llandovery
Tel. 01550 720693

Merthyr Tydfil
Tel. 01685 379884

Pont Nedd Fechan
Tel. 01639 721795

National Park Visitor Centres:
Abergavenny
Swan Meadow, Monmouth Road
Abergavenny NP7 5ER
Tel. 01873 853254

Brecon
Cattle Market Car Park,
Brecon LD3 9DA
Tel. 01874 623156

Craig-y-Nos Country Park
Brecon Road, Penycae,
Swansea Valley SA9 1GL
Tel. 01639 730395

Llandovery
The Heritage Centre,
Llandovery SA20 0AW
Tel. 01550 720693

National Park Visitor Centre (Mountain Centre)
Libanus, Brecon,
Powys LD3 7DP
Tel. 01874 623366

Public Transport
For all public transport enquiries:
Bus Traveline
Tel. 0870 6082608

National Rail Enquiries
Tel. 08457 484950

Answers to Questions
Walk 1: Three.
Walk 2: Y Fenni.
Walk 3: Y Deri Fach.
Walk 4: They do not lose their leaves in the winter.
Walk 5: A reservoir is man-made.
Walk 6: Shire horses.
Walk 7: Because they are easier to defend.
Walk 8: An aqueduct.
Walk 9: ——
Walk 10: It's called Whitewalls but is actually made of stone and red in colour.
Walk 11: Nineteen.
Walk 12: ——
Walk 13: Six metres.
Walk 14: Oak trees.
Walk 15: The middle one, Pen y Fan.
Walk 16: ——
Walk 17: Look at the plinth in the car park if you need help.
Walk 18: England.
Walk 19: ——
Walk 20: September 2.

Rainbow over Glyntawe